EXTRA JOY DINARY

EXTRA JOY DINARY

creating your serene life

A Self-Help Project of
The ExtraJOYdinary
Writers Group

EXTRA**JOY**DINARY: creating your serene life. Copyright © 2017, 2025 by Tullisian Books. All rights reserved. The unauthorized reproduction and/or distribution of this book is strictly prohibited. If you would like to use material from this book (other than for review purposes), prior written permission must be obtained by contacting the publisher.

Published by
Tullisian Books
Little Rock Arkansas
TullisianBooks@davidolintullis.com

Extra**JOY**dinary™ is a trademark created and owned by David Olin Tullis since 2011.

ISBN-13: 978-0-9979127-5-3 (Softcover)

Date of first US publication: May 3, 2017
Date of Re-release: April 25, 2025

Table of Contents

Publisher's Introduction – Page 1
Chapter One – Page 9
Chapter Two – Page 15
Chapter Three – Page 19
Chapter Four – Page 23
Chapter Five – Page 27
Chapter Six – Page 31
Chapter Seven – Page 35
Chapter Eight – Page 39
Chapter Nine – Page 45
Chapter Ten – Page 49
Chapter Eleven – Page 53
Chapter Twelve – Page 61
Chapter Thirteen – Page 69
Chapter Fourteen – Page 75
Chapter Fifteen – Page 81
Afterword – Page 87

Publisher's Introduction

> "There's always room to be a better person. Always."
>
> — Sonya Teclai

Simply reading this book is not likely to change your life. It was written to give you the inspiration you may need to change and correct the parts of your life that are preventing you from living a serene and extraJOYdinary life. You must do all the work.

Before you begin your own journey, I would like to give you some background information about the journey that made this book possible.

In 2008, I commissioned Cecil Witherspoon to write "New Branches on the Family Tree," the third in a series of books known collectively as The Sara, the Pineapple Cat Children's Book Collection. Here is the biography that he wrote for the book.

> Cecil Witherspoon (author) is a 33-year-old freelance writer, artist, and craftsman. He lives a serene life on a Missouri farm with his partner of twelve years.
>
> "New Branches on the Family Tree" is Cecil's first children's book – but certainly not his last.
>
> Mr. Witherspoon is currently working on a book for adults and teenagers entitled "Beyond Joy – Creating Your Serene Life."

The following year, Cecil co-authored "Sara, the Pineapple Cat's Alphabet Book." Here is the biography that he submitted for the second book.

> Cecil Witherspoon is a thirty-four year old freelance writer, artist, and craftsman. He lives a serene life on a Missouri farm with his partner of thirteen years.

A gentleman purchased "Sara, the Pineapple Cat's Alphabet Book" for his daughter. While reading the book with her, he was intrigued by the biography. Unaware of Mr. Witherspoon's one-time plan to write "Beyond Joy," the man wrote to me suggesting that I publish a book written by Cecil on how to live a serene life. Never having heard anyone describe their life as serene, he thought it would make a good book. I agree.

I must point out that, although this book was inspired by the life of Cecil Witherspoon, he did not participate in the writing of it. It was done with his blessing, though. The actual writers agreed that, rather than being known individually, they want to be known collectively as The ExtraJOYdinary Writers Group.

~~To make the most of this project, you will need a copy of "My Life is Extra~~JOY~~dinary – The Workbook." This book contains the forms that you will need to plan and document your journey.~~

~~You may be wondering why the forms were not included in this book. I agree that it would have been easier. However, this book can (and, hopefully, will be) shared with other people. Your workbook is personal and confidential and should not be shared with anyone. This is your personal and private journey.~~

~~Treat your workbook carefully. Treat your life carefully. They are each important and valuable.~~

~~It is our recommendation that you read your workbook every day. It should be a constant reminder that everything you do and everything you say should represent the extra~~JOY~~dinary person that you want to be.~~

You will notice that we have included a few of our favorite quotations in this book. (The people whose quotations we used are not affiliated with this book, in any way.) My personal mantra for this year is "Nothing changes if nothing changes." I do not know who said it first, but I thank him/her. It is currently guiding my life. We are constantly inspired, not only by the actual quotations, but by some people's ability to use so few words to say so very much. We used that as a guide in writing this book. It was intentionally written as simply as possible. This is not a novel. There is no story. The real story, to be told later by you, is the story of your extraJOYdinary life.

    I wish each of you a serene and extraJOYdinary life.

Chapter One

"The difference between who you are and who you want to be is what you do."

Unknown

One member of our writers group published his first non-fiction book in 2003. Like other authors, he hoped and prayed that his many readers would find his writing entertaining, inspiring, and enlightening. It was he who found enlightenment when asked to write his own author biography.

How does one summarize their entire life in just a few sentences? It was something to which he gave much thought. As difficult as it was for him, he was pleased with the final seven sentence, two paragraph, results.

He found the process so meaningful that he began encouraging his non-writer friends to write their own biographies. It is interesting what people consider important enough to include and unimportant enough to leave out.

His experience, coupled with the fact that this book was inspired by an author biography, leads us to our first exercise.

Whether or not you actually are a writer, let's pretend that you are. Your first book has just been accepted for publication. The last thing you need to write is your own author biography. Using the suggested length of seven sentences and two paragraphs, use Form [A] to write your biography. Remember, every word must be true. No exaggerations or embellishments.

For the second part of this exercise, you must pretend that your life, up to this point, is everything you always wanted it to be. Every (realistic) dream has come true. Every (realistic) goal has been achieved. Your first book has just been accepted for publication and you must write your own author biography. Using the same suggested length, use Form [B] to write your perfect life biography.

The third and final part of this exercise is to figure out how to get from Form [A] to Form [B]. It can be done. When you are walking, it takes individual steps to get you where you want to go. In life, it also takes individual steps to get you where you want to be. Think about the person you want to be – the person you described on Form [B]. Using Form [C] write down the individual steps you need to take to become that person. Write each step on a separate form and use as many forms as needed.

Our dreams and our goals are subject to change. If you find that your life needs to take a different direction from the one you wrote about on Form [B], complete a new Form [B] at any time. This will probably require the addition and subtraction of steps on Form [C]. Make the necessary adjustments, but remain steady in your journey for self-improvement.

We would like to offer a suggestion for your first Form [C] goal. Be kind. Not just kinder, but truly kind. Make a conscious effort to only speak kind words, to only write kind words, and to only do kind things. Even if this is the only thing you change in your life, this book will have been worthwhile.

Chapter Two

"Actions prove who someone is. Words just prove who they want to be."

Unknown

Your dreams and your goals are important. Specifically, they are important to you. They don't become important to other people until they have been accomplished.

When people ask you about your dreams and aspirations, they are not asking out of concern. They are asking out of curiosity. When you voluntarily offer information about your goals, you are simply giving them a reason to criticize you.

It is best not to speak about what you are going to do. Talk only about your goals that you are actually working toward or have successfully accomplished.

Chapter Three

"Watch your thoughts, for they become words. Watch your words, for they become actions. Watch your actions, for they become habits. Watch your habits, for they become character. Watch your character, for it becomes your destiny."

Unknown

Only by being the best person that we can be are we able to live a serene and extraJOYdinary life. We all have habits and traits that diminish us as human beings and prevent us from being the person that we should be. It would be impossible to list all of these habits and traits, but here are a few of the most common.

Overindulgence in food or drink.

Misuse of over-the-counter or prescription drugs or use of any recreational drug.

Use of any tobacco or nicotine product.

Use of profanity.

Unkind behavior (words or actions).

Telling lies or spreading unconfirmed rumors.

Overspending or any financial impropriety.

Untidy behavior (yourself or surroundings).

Unreliability or poor work ethics.

Sexually promiscuous or indiscriminate.

The list is endless.

Some traits will be easy to recognize and relatively easy to correct. Begin with those. Other traits will be easy to recognize, but difficult to correct. Please don't give up. To rid yourself and your life of these unwanted and unnecessary behaviors will not only improve your life, but the lives of those around you.

For each habit or trait that you wish to change, list it on Form [D]. List each one individually and use as many forms as necessary.

Now is the time to make some serious changes in your life. We all have room for improvement. Begin now. Your future self will be grateful.

Chapter Four

> "Maturing is realizing how many things don't require your comment."
>
> — Rachel Wolchin

Yes, we are each entitled to our own opinions – if our opinions do not contradict the truth. A fact is a fact. Having an opinion, however, does not give us the right to share it under just any circumstance. If you are specifically and individually asked for your opinion, you may freely share it. The most appropriate time to offer your opinion is when you are actually having a conversation with someone. Even then, you don't have to, but it would be acceptable. Otherwise, any time you offer your unsolicited opinion, verbal or written, know that the recipients of your wisdom are thinking "try to imagine how little I care" or something much more unprintable.

The least appropriate times to offer your opinions are online comment sections. These sections, if fact, should not even exist. It is acceptable to offer a compliment online (always be kind), but other comments should be avoided. The same rule should apply to letters to the (newspaper) editor. If you wish to offer a writer or photographer a compliment, by all means do so. However, your general opinions about life are never welcome.

Chapter Five

> "Nothing will bring you greater peace than minding your own business."
>
> Unknown

Even two hundred twenty-seven years after his death, Benjamin Franklin (1706 – 1790) is still remembered for his accomplishments, his intelligence, and his wisdom.

In 1787, the Congress of the Confederation of the United States authorized a design for an official copper penny. This coin, designed by Benjamin Franklin, was later referred to as the "Fugio cent." As a reminder to its holders, he put at its bottom the message, "Mind Your Business." These words, along with an image on the coin, form a rebus that means "time flies, do your work."

Because Mr. Franklin was an influential and successful businessman, some historians believe that his use of the word "business" was intended literally. Others believe, probably more truthfully, that it may have meant both monetary and social business.

Both meanings are relevant today and they are relevant to everyone.

"Mind your business" and do your work.

"Mind your business" and do not interfere with people and things that do not concern you.

Chapter Six

"Compliment people. Magnify their strengths, not their weaknesses."

Unknown

Compliments. Beautiful words that just make us feel good all over. Everyone loves receiving compliments. However, we probably receive more compliments than we should and give fewer than we should. Be generous with your kind words, but always be sincere and truthful.

This exercise requires you to think back over your life and try to remember (it shouldn't be difficult) the unexpected compliments that mean the most to you. Maybe it was the compliment itself that was unexpected, or maybe it was the source of the compliment that made it unexpected and memorable.

Using Form [E], write each compliment on a separate sheet. Write it as precisely as you remember it. Be sure to include the source of the compliment.

That is the extent of the written part of this exercise. Read your workbook daily and remind yourself of what you must do to live up to the kind thoughts that people have of you. View each compliment as a goal. Some people's lives are changed forever by a single compliment.

Chapter Seven

> "The hardest job kids face today is learning good manners without seeing any."
>
> Fred Astaire

From the day we are born until the day we die, it is our own responsibility to learn and to educate ourselves. There are people, officially and unofficially, who share their knowledge with us and guide us to learn, but it is ultimately up to us to do the work. Never stop reading. Never stop listening. Open your mind. Learn as much as you can about as many things as you can. You will never be an expert on every subject. That should not be your goal. Try to be an expert on the things that are important in your life, but never come across to other people as an "expert." We all know people like that, don't we? Your goal is to be as well-rounded as possible.

One area of our education that is important to everyone, but generally neglected by everyone, is etiquette. Etiquette extends far beyond table manners, although that is very important.

Fortunately, there are etiquette books that will guide you in every aspect of your life.

There are etiquette books specifically for children, teen-agers, and adults. There are books for men and books for women. There are books that deal with workplace etiquette and books that deal with at-home etiquette. There are excellent books about foreign travel and what is expected of you – and what is not accepted in other cultures. Find the books that apply to you and add them to your permanent library. Refer to them often.

Chapter Eight

"Evil lurks in places you would never imagine and tries to charm its way into your life."

Unknown

Have you ever looked – really looked closely – at abandoned buildings? Some are just sad. It is easy to just jump to the conclusion that they should be demolished. Others, though, are quite beautiful. There is an elegance and grace about them.

You can look at an abandoned house and think about the wonderful things that once took place there. Family dinners every night in the kitchen. Festive holiday dinners in the dining room. Lovemaking in the master bedroom. Bedrooms painted in pastel colors for the nursery and repainted as the children grew up.

Walk through an abandoned church building and imagine the beautiful music from the choir and the musical instruments. Listen carefully and you can imagine hearing the inspirational sermons given every Sunday by the minister.

Likewise, when you see an abandoned storefront, you can imagine all the hustle and bustle of shoppers and the ringing of the cash registers as the clerks completed the sales.

The buildings that we would actually like to see abandoned are our jails and prisons. Can you imagine everyone in the world living their life as it should be lived? Honest. Respectful. Peaceful. Try to imagine all of our jails and prisons completely deserted. Those people could then live in the restored abandoned houses, work in the restored storefronts, and sing and worship in all of the restored churches. If everyone, absolutely everyone, made the effort to live an extraJOYdinary life, that is the world we would have.

This is, perhaps, the most personal chapter/exercise of all. It requires you to take a long, hard look at yourself and face your demons. We all have them. You are not alone.

Evil exists in each of us. Obviously, to varying degrees. Only you know how much power Evil has over your life – and also how much power Good has over your life.

It may not be easy, but for this exercise you must put a number value for each one. On Form [F], use a scale from 1 through 9 to rate the Good and the Evil in you. The two numbers must equal ten. The very best that any of us can be is Good = 9 and Evil = 1. Likewise, the most evil among us would be rated Good = 1 and Evil = 9. On the same Form [F], write the reasons for the ratings you gave yourself.

This form alone will be reason enough to keep your workbook private.

Use multiple copies of Form [G] to write the individual steps that you need to make to improve your ratings. This will include the things you need to do, as well as the things you must stop doing. Use a separate form for each step. Remember, the goal for everyone should be Good = 9 and Evil = 1.

Chapter Nine

"Don't be busy. Be productive."

Unknown

Time is one of our most precious assets. We should treat it with the same respect as we do our money. Like money, we never truly know how much we have remaining. We only know how much we have already used.

It is possible to stay busy all the time and actually accomplish little or nothing at all. Obviously, that is not how we should spend our time, especially if we are being paid for our time.

Try to be productive and actually accomplish things that are worthwhile. The feeling you get when you have completed a worthwhile task is unlike any other.

The point of this is that we should make thoughtful and conscious decisions about how we spend our time, which is ultimately how we spend our lives.

Chapter Ten

> "If you feel like a tourist in the city you were born, then it's time to go."
>
> Unknown

Some people spend their entire lives on the same farm or in the same town or city in which they grew up. Some people go to the college that was selected for them by their parents or other well-meaning person. Some people follow the career path that was selected for them – or expected of time.

Some people get married because it is expected of them or because it makes someone else happy. Some people have children simply because their parents want grandchildren or because they are expected to carry on the family name.

The biggest regrets in life are probably caused by following a path that was chosen for you, not by you. You will never live a serene and joyful life unless you follow your own path. Live your own life. Follow your own dreams. Find success your own way.

Chapter Eleven

> "He who buys what he does not need steals from himself."
>
> Swedish Proverb

Money is a funny thing. Everyone wants money – lots of money. That's fine, to a degree, because everyone needs money to survive.

Most people, it seems, don't have a healthy view of money. We look up to people who have money. They more money they have, the higher the pedestal we put them on. It doesn't even matter how they made their money. People who have money are viewed as smarter, more talented, and harder workers than other people. They're not, at least not always. People who don't have much money are often viewed as people who don't work hard enough and are not as smart as other people. That is not necessarily true, either.

This book is not a guide for getting rich. We are not financial planners. But we have all learned a few things about money and we would like to share our experiences with you. Most people will benefit from at least some of our recommendations.

- We opened this chapter with the Swedish Proverb, "He who buys what he does not need steals from himself." Truer words were never spoken. Don't waste your money.
- Most people think that their home is their biggest expense. Remember, though, that the cost of raising each child is, generally speaking, the same as buying another house. Can you afford multiple homes?
- When every child is born, the parents, grandparents, whomever, should open an interest-bearing retirement account for that child. Money can be added to the account at any time. However, no amount of money, no matter how small, can be withdrawn from the account prior to that person's retirement. This is one of our favorite ideas.
- From a person's very first paycheck to the very last one, a percentage of that check should be deposited into a retirement account. We have been unable to find the

exact quote, but Eva Gabor once said something like, "To grow old is inevitable. To be old and poor is inexcusable." We couldn't agree more.
- Likewise, when every child is born, the parents, grandparents, whomever, should open an interest-bearing college account for that child. Just like the retirement account, money can be added to the account at any time, but absolutely no withdrawals prior to the child reaching college age.
- While we are on the subject of college, do not, under any circumstances, rely on student loans to finance someone's higher education. If the parents are unable to fully pay for college, the student should work his/her way through college. Of course, one should always take advantage of any scholarships and other financial offerings. The student (and parents) should be debt-free on graduation day.

- One should always have at least two sources of income. A full-time job and a home-based business, for example. Perhaps a hobby that can also generate income. Owning rental property is also a good source of additional income. People are very creative and imaginative when it comes of business ideas. Think about what interests you and go for it.
- Every responsible adult should have at least one credit card. It is almost essential in the world we live in today. However, there are certain guidelines that we recommend. First of all, use a credit card that offers some type of reward – airline miles, cash back, etc. Always pay your account in full each month. You should never have to pay interest charges to the credit card company. Think of your credit card(s) as a convenience, not as a way to buy something you cannot afford.
- Many people can benefit from the expertise of a certified and licensed

financial planner. Let them use their expertise to guide your decisions, but never give anyone total control of your money. It is your money. How it is managed is ultimately your responsibility.
- Remember, there is enough money in this world for everyone to be rich. Just because you don't have a lot of money now doesn't mean that it has to be that way for your entire life. You are only limited by your own insecurities. The more imaginative and hard-working you are, the wealthier you can become. Just make sure that every dollar you earn is obtained honestly.

Chapter Twelve

> "Spectacular achievement is always preceded by unspectacular preparation."
>
> Robert H. Schuller

Life is like Thanksgiving dinner (or any large family feast for those of you who do not celebrate Thanksgiving). Just like any other large task, Thanksgiving requires a lot of planning and hard work to achieve the desired results. And, trust us, life is a large task, too. It certainly requires a lot of planning and hard work to achieve the desired results.

Let's break it down and see just how similar they are.

After you have decided to host a Thanksgiving dinner, there are many decisions to be made. Who will you invite? What time will you serve dinner? What food will you serve? What dishes will you use? What decorations, if any, will you have? What do you already have and what will you need to buy? Write it down. It's easy to forget.

You may plan to use "the good stuff" that you haven't used since you hosted Thanksgiving last year. Are the dishes clean?

Are the tablecloth and napkins spot-free and pressed? If not, get to work.

Thanksgiving is all about the food. What are you going to cook? The same things you always serve or are you going to try something new? Do you need to gather any recipes together or do you have it all memorized? Make your shopping list. What is already in your pantry? What do you need to buy?

Did you write it all down? Try to get your shopping done in one trip. Why have to go back just for that one item you forgot?

All of the planning and preparation for Thanksgiving dinner represents your life from birth until the end of your formal education. Of course, birth is the same for everyone. The end of your formal education varies greatly. Everyone has to decide for themselves just how long they want or need to go to school, but we do have a few things to say about it.

Unless a person has physical or mental challenges that prevent it, every person should graduate from high school. This is the absolute minimum for education. No matter how many excuses some people try to make for dropping out of school, there is no excuse for failing to graduate from high school. None.

With that high school diploma in your hand, you now have many options. No college. Two year college. Four year college. Technical or vocational school. Graduate school. Your career choice will often make the decision for you. First you learn, then you earn. Remember that.

Speaking of career choice, one of the biggest mistakes you can make in life is not to have one. Many people do it, but please do not be content with just finding a job. It may lead you to finding your true calling, but it will probably never lead you to anything more than a minimal paycheck.

Decide for yourself what you want to do with your life. Plan for it. Educate yourself for it. Then do it. If you don't do what you love, then you may just hate what you are doing.

Now that the pre-Thanksgiving Day preparations are complete, it is time to actually prepare, serve, and enjoy this wonderful meal with your family and friends. This section stops just before dessert is served.

The period of your life that relates to this begins at the end of your formal education and the beginning of your career. This is actually the best time in your life. This should be when all the good stuff happens. You have a career that you love. You're making good money. Maybe this is when you get married and possibly have a family. Life is good.

We have already established our love of brilliant quotations. This is one of the most brilliant. It was written by Jeanne Phillips, who is known to the world as Dear Abby. "It's my observation that people with little life experience tend to be judgmental about things they know nothing about."

By the time you have reached this point in your life, you should have much life experience and should be judgmental about pretty much nothing. Not being judgmental will greatly increase the amount of joy and serenity in your life – and in the lives of the people around you.

Thanksgiving dinner typically ends with dessert. After that comes the less enjoyable task of cleaning up and putting everything in its rightful place.

This corresponds to your life from the first day of retirement until the last day of your life. Your retirement should be a sweet time in your life when you savor every moment. But there is always the "getting your affairs in order" time. Just like Thanksgiving dinner, the more clean-up that you do as you go along, the less you have to do at the end.

Of course, not everyone lives long enough to enjoy "dessert." That's why it is so very important to make the most of every moment in your life. Plan for the future, but live for today.

Chapter Thirteen

> "Make a habit of two things: to help, or at least to do no harm."
>
> Unknown

Many (most?) people dream of creating something or doing something that continues to live on long after they are gone. Hippocrates may have had this dream, but we doubt that even he thought that his Hippocratic Oath, believed to have been written by him in the late Fifth Century BC, would still be in use today.

The Hippocratic Oath was written for doctors and, even today, is taken by some doctors. But we asked ourselves, why shouldn't there be an Oath that is suitable for everyone? So we have created The ExtraJOYdinary Oath for everyone. You will find a signable copy of it on Form [H]. We hope that you will take this Oath and do your very best to live up to it. (Full-color posters for your home or office, framed and unframed, are available for purchase.)

The ExtraJOYdinary Oath

I swear to fulfill, to the best of my ability and judgment, this covenant:

- I will show kindness to everyone in all that I say, write, and do.
- I will live my entire life in the way in which my biography reflects not only the life I lived, but the life I chose to live.
- I will speak of my goals and ambitions only while actually achieving my goals and ambitions. Idle dreams are not worth talking about.
- I will recognize my own negative behaviors and rid my life of them.
- I will speak only when it is appropriate to do so and I will share my opinions only when asked.
- I will not get involved with, or concern myself in any way, with people and issues which do not involve or affect me.
- I will live a life of productivity and accomplishment.

- I will follow my own path, not a path that was chosen for me.
- I will treat my assets and resources with respect and live a life of financial responsibility.
- I realize that successful outcomes require appropriate education and preparation. I will do what is necessary to achieve success in all endeavors.
- I will do no harm to this planet or to its inhabitants.
- I will work to do or to create something that will live on after I am gone and represent my life in a positive way.
- I will leave this world knowing that I lived a life of beauty and purpose.

Chapter Fourteen

> "We all die. The goal isn't to live forever, the goal is to create something that will."
>
> Unknown

The recommendations in this book come from many sources. Most of them are based on the personal experiences and imagination of our writers. The remaining exercises were inspired by things that we have heard or read.

This exercise comes from a Sunday afternoon of one of our writers. It is, quite possibly, our favorite.

As with most theatre-goers, this writer has his favorite Broadway show. If he were to list his top ten shows, there would have be a large gap between the number one and the number two positions. This one show is very important to him and it has, in fact, strongly influenced his life – for the better – for many years. He has actually seen the show live at least two dozen times, in five different states. Many of the songs from the show have been recorded by multiple artists. He owns many of these recordings. The entire show has never been filmed, but there are DVDs of concert versions of the show. And that brings us to that fateful Sunday afternoon.

A spectacular anniversary concert version of the show had been performed. He was not in attendance, much to his regret, but as soon as a DVD of the show was released, he placed an online order for it. It was delivered on a Sunday afternoon.

It had, up until that point, been a very quiet Sunday afternoon. With much excitement and without hesitation, he opened the package, carefully removed the DVD, and gently placed it in the DVD player.

For the next two-plus hours, he was in another world, totally transfixed and inspired by what he heard and saw. He was so happy that he smiled with sheer joy, even as tears rolled down his cheeks.

Although he did not want it to end, the magnificent finale ended, the credits rolled across the screen, and he sat there exhausted, exhilarated, and inspired.

He actually spoke out loud, to an empty room, and made the promise to himself that before he dies, he will create something that is as wonderful as the show that he had just experienced.

It was never his intention to write a Broadway show, although everyone who knows him would probably agree that he could if he wanted to. His intention is to leave behind something – anything – that is so wonderful that the world actually is a better place for his being here.

Why can't his goal be everyone's goal?

Give it a great deal of thought. It may not come to you immediately. Using Form [K], write down the one man-made creation on this Earth that you think is the most beautiful, the most wonderful, the most inspirational ever created.

Think carefully about your own talents, even the ones that you have never utilized. We all have more talents than we use. What do you want to create, and share with the world, that is just as beautiful, just as wonderful, and just as inspirational as what you wrote on Form [K]? Write it down.

Make a plan. When can you start? When would you like to finish and present your creation? Don't procrastinate. The world is waiting.

Chapter Fifteen

> "When it comes time to die, let us not discover that we have never lived."
>
> Henry David Thoreau

Our final chapter is, appropriately enough, about your obituary. Please do not think that we are ending this book on a sad note. There should be nothing sad about a death unless it comes at the end of a life that was not well-lived. We hope that everyone, especially those who follow our process, have lives that are well-lived.

We actually like the idea of writing one's own obituary. There may need to be minor changes made before it is published, but don't you really want to have the last word?

This final step in our process is a lot like the first one. For this exercise, please use Form [L] and write your obituary as it would appear if you passed away today. Please be truthful and accurate.

Use Form [M] to write your "ideal" obituary, the one you hope will be published – at a much later date, of course.

Using multiple copies of Form [N], write the steps needed to take your life from what it is to the well-lived life you hope to leave behind.

Have you ever noticed that people become practically perfect after they die? They become more attractive and more intelligent. Their smiles become bigger and brighter. Their friends become much more devoted to them. They become more successful. They become less guilty of any wrong-doing. They become morally superior to the rest of us who are still living. They just become all-around better people than anyone ever thought they were when they were alive. Of course, they don't really become any of these things. But people often talk about them as if they did. The point of this is that we should all live our lives in a way that if anyone ever says something negative about us after we die, no one will believe them.

We would like to share with you an actual quote from a news article. We are not going to identify the subject of the article, though. It is one of the saddest things we have ever read.

"Xxxxx's still alive, though she's never apologized or expressed regret. Reflecting back on the impact she's had and her lingering, now-funny legacy, it must be hard not to feel like a waste of a life."

Please do not waste your life. Be the type of person you know you should be and encourage everyone you know to do the same.

Afterword

> "If you've made your point, stop talking."
>
> — Unknown

www.ingramcontent.com/pod-product-compliance
Lightning Source LLC
Chambersburg PA
CBHW051551010526
44118CB00022B/2667